M000072897

ed her to the finest ice
ad to offer, our dinner
rb. I kissed her, and it
hocolate."

— PRESIDENT BARACK OBAMA
RVIEW IN *O, THE OPRAH MAGAZINE*, FEB. 2007;
IMAGE COURTESY OF BLACKPAST.ORG

na first kissed Michelle Obama.

THIS BOOK BELONGS TO

_____

13-Digit ISBN: 978-1604337839
10-Digit ISBN: 1604337834

This book may be ordered by mail from the publisher. Please include $5.99 for postage and handling. Please support your local bookseller first! Books published by Cider Mill Press Book Publishers are available at special discounts for bulk purchases in the United States by corporations, institutions, and other organizations. For more information, please contact the publisher.

Cider Mill Press Book Publishers
"Where good books are ready for press"
PO Box 454
12 Spring Street
Kennebunkport, Maine 04046
Visit us online! www.cidermillpress.com

Typography: Bauer Bodoni, Georgia and Voluta
Image credits: Michelle Obama's signature (Wikimedia Commons); front endpapers: Official Portrait of First Lady Michelle Obama by Joyce N. Boghosian, February 18, 2009 (Library of Congress Prints and Photographs Division LC-DIG-ppbd- 00357); back endpapers: Official portrait of First Lady Michelle Obama in the Green Room of the White House by Chuck Kennedy, February 12, 2013 (Library of Congress Prints and Photographs Division Washington LC-DIG-ppbd-00604); all other images used under license from Shutterstock.

Printed in China
4 5 6 7 8

MICHELLE OBAMA

SIGNATURE EDITION

CIDER MILL
PRESS

BOOK
PUBLISHERS
KENNEBUNKPORT, MAINE

Introduction

BY DAVID COLBERT, AUTHOR OF *MICHELLE OBAMA: AN AMERICAN LIFE*

*I*n the decade since most Americans first met Michelle Obama, she has become both an icon to be admired from a distance, and one of the few public figures we feel we know as well as we know our friends.

This connection blossomed before her husband, Barack Obama, won the Presidency. She cut right through the cynicism of the campaign trail. We saw and trusted that the warm, energetic, and funny woman we met during the campaign was the genuine Michelle.

By the time she left the White House, she had exceeded our highest hopes and expectations. We saw her navigate the most vicious, personal politics in living memory with grace, dignity, and confidence.

While people questioned the most obvious and basic truths about her and her family, she remained positive. She focused on what needed to get done. Her strength is inspirational.

Barack inspires people to believe in what they can achieve. He changed history when he was elected. He accomplished something other presidents couldn't when he secured Obamacare for Americans. Michelle inspires us in a different way. She makes us believe in what we can be. The essence of every speech she made as First Lady were ideas that have guided her since she was a child. The highest achievement is simply to be the best version of ourselves. We'll change our worlds if we try to do only that.

For Michelle, trying has always meant the same thing: facing the challenges that make her uncomfortable. She has been doing it since before she saw the pattern. She chose to go to an academically tough high school in Chicago far from her neighborhood. The trip took an hour and a half on two city buses, each way. A teacher later observed, "When [Michelle] applied and came here, the tradition of leaving one's neighborhood to go to high school was very new, and a person had to be very gutsy to do it." Princeton University and Harvard Law were more of the same. In one of her early jobs, she found herself, at age thirty, managing a diverse group of young people who hadn't spent much time with people who were different. She helped them find common ground by emphasizing honesty over politeness. "Real change," she later explained, "comes from having enough comfort to be really honest and say something very uncomfortable."

The comfort to be uncomfortable. Where does it come from? It's not overconfidence. She admitted that before the first campaign, "I took myself down every dark road you could go on, just to prepare myself before we jumped out there." It comes from her parents—a courageous father who battled a severe disability yet never stopped working, and a mother who showed Michelle how to excel at school while following her heart. She learned to think through all the details but then to take them one at a time. She isn't overwhelmed by the collective weight of them. She knows there's no straight line from start to finish. She expects mistakes. In fact, some of the most admired parts of her biography— Princeton University, Harvard Law—are things she once questioned deeply, when they sent her in the direction of corporate law instead of public service. She has also learned that she'll be misunderstood by some people, and that being misunderstood isn't a reason to stop.

Whether you've picked up this notebook to start a new creative project or to get control of the details in your life, the temptation is to want success to come magically. The lesson of Michelle's life is that magic doesn't happen from magical thinking. You don't wish yourself into the stars. You climb there, one rung at a time, one task at a time, one idea at a time, one page at a time. Turn the page and start, and enjoy it when it gets tough.

We have an obligation to

fight

for the world as it should be.

—*2008 Democratic National Convention* (August 25, 2008)

It is our fundamental belief in the

power of hope

that has allowed us to rise above the
voices of doubt and division,
of anger and fear.

—*Final remarks as First Lady while honoring the 2017 School
Counselor of the Year (January 6, 2017)*

*Michelle Obama campaigning for presidential candidate Barack
Obama in Asheville, North Carolina (May 2, 2008)*

In all the noise that you hear, there's always a voice of power and *beauty and positivity.* Each and every one of you, if you think about it, no matter what negativity you hear, there is always some ray of positive hope out there that you can choose to take in.

—*Remarks at a White House screening of* Hidden Figures
(December 15, 2016)

True

leadership often happens with the smallest acts, in the most unexpected places, by the most unlikely individuals.

—Keynote Address at Young African Women Leaders Forum
(June 22, 2011)

First Lady Michelle Obama at the opening of the Anna Wintour Costume Center at the Metropolitan Museum of Art (May 5, 2014)

As a child, my first doll was Malibu Barbie. That was the standard for perfection. That was what the world told me to aspire to. But then I discovered Maya Angelou, and her words

lifted me right out of my own little head.

—*Remarks at the memorial service for Dr. Maya Angelou*
(June 7, 2014)

Michelle Obama and President-Elect Barack Obama with daughters Sasha and Malia after the President-Elect's Victory Speech in Chicago, Illinois (November 4, 2008)

Today, when the challenges we face start to seem overwhelming – or even impossible – let us never forget that

doing the impossible is the history of this nation

...it's who we are as Americans...it's how this country was built.

—2012 Democratic National Convention (September 4, 2012)

Don't be afraid.

Be focused.
Be determined.

Be hopeful. Be empowered.

*—Final remarks as First Lady while honoring the 2017 School
Counselor of the Year* (January 6, 2017)

*Michelle Obama campaigning for presidential candidate
Barack Obama at UCLA in Los Angeles, California*
(February 3, 2008)

Never view your challenges
as a disadvantage....
your experience
*facing and
overcoming
adversity*
is actually one of your
biggest advantages.

—*Commencement Address at City College of New York*
(June 3, 2016)

Don't just tell people that
you love them, show them.
And that means showing up.
It means being

truly present

in the lives of the people
you care about.

—*Commencement Address at Oregon University* (June 17, 2012)

*First Lady Michelle Obama and President Barack Obama
at a commemoration of the 50th anniversary of the March
on Washington* (August 28, 2013)

I never cut class.

I loved getting A's, I liked being
smart. I liked being on time.
I thought being smart is cooler
than anything in the world.

—*Address to schoolgirls at Elizabeth Garrett Anderson School
during the G20 London Summit* (April 2, 2009)

When you've worked hard, and done well, and walked through that doorway of opportunity, you do not slam it shut behind you.

You reach back.

— *2012 Democratic National Convention* (September 4, 2012)

First Lady Michelle Obama after delivering a speech at the University of Illinois at Chicago (October 7, 2014)

First Lady Michelle Obama at a White House event marking the 25th anniversary of National Breast Cancer Awareness Month (October 23, 2009)

Seek out the most contentious, polarized, gridlocked places you can find. Because so often, throughout our history, those have been the places where progress really happens — the places where

minds are changed, lives transformed,

where our great American story unfolds.

—Commencement Address at Oberlin College (May 25, 2015)

There will never be a point at
which people will one-hundred
percent be cheering you on.
So when you hit those barriers
in life,

all you have is
your belief in
yourself.

—*Remarks at a White House screening of* Hidden Figures
(December 15, 2016)

First Lady Michelle Obama at a public appearance for the Afternoon Tea Honoring Women in the Military, held at the White House (November 19, 2009)

Success

isn't about how your life
looks to others, it's about
how it feels to you.

—Commencement Address at Oregon University
(June 17, 2012)

*First Lady Michelle Obama lands in Milan to visit Expo 2015,
along with daughters Sasha and Malia and mother Marian
Robinson* (June 16, 2015)

People who are truly strong

lift others up.

People who are truly powerful
bring others together.

—*Speech at a campaign rally in Manchester, New Hampshire*
(October 13, 2016)

We want our children — and all children in this nation — to know that the only limit to the height of your achievements is the

reach of your dreams

and your willingness to work for them.

—*2008 Democratic National Convention*
(August 25, 2008)

First Lady Michelle Obama and President Barack Obama acknowledge the crowd after the President's farewell address in Chicago, Illinois (January 10, 2017)

That is the

power of our differences,

to make us smarter and
more creative.

—*Commencement Address at City College of New York*
(June 3, 2016)

There are still so many causes worth sacrificing for. There is still

so much history yet to be made.

—*Keynote Address at Young African Women Leaders Forum* (June 22, 2011)

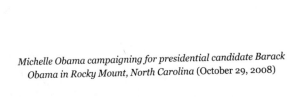

Michelle Obama campaigning for presidential candidate Barack Obama in Rocky Mount, North Carolina (October 29, 2008)

No matter what struggles or
setbacks you face in your life,

*focus on what
you have,*

not on what you're missing.

—*Commencement Address at Oregon University* (June 17, 2012)

You cannot take your freedoms
for granted. Just like generations
who have come before you,
you have to do your part to

preserve and protect

those freedoms.

*—Final remarks as First Lady while honoring the 2017 School
Counselor of the Year (January 6, 2017)*

*First Lady Michelle Obama after visiting the British Prime
Minister residence in London, England (June 15, 2016)*

I am an example of what is possible when girls from the very beginning of their lives are **_loved and nurtured_** by people around them. I was surrounded by extraordinary women in my life who taught me about quiet strength and dignity.

—*Address to schoolgirls at Elizabeth Garrett Anderson School during the G20 London Summit (April 2, 2009)*

First Lady Michelle Obama at a campaign rally in Philadelphia, Pennsylvania (September 27, 2016)

First Lady Michelle Obama at a campaign event in Winston-Salem, North Carolina (October 27, 2016)

About Cider Mill Press
Book Publishers

Good ideas ripen with time. From seed to harvest,
Cider Mill Press brings fine reading, information,
and entertainment together between the covers
of its creatively crafted books. Our Cider Mill
bears fruit twice a year, publishing a new crop
of titles each spring and fall.

**BOOK
PUBLISHERS**

"Where Good Books Are Ready for Press"

Visit us on the Web at
www.cidermillpress.com
or write to us at
PO Box 454
12 Spring St.
Kennebunkport, Maine 04046